Farm Friends

Match.

Gone Fishing

Match.

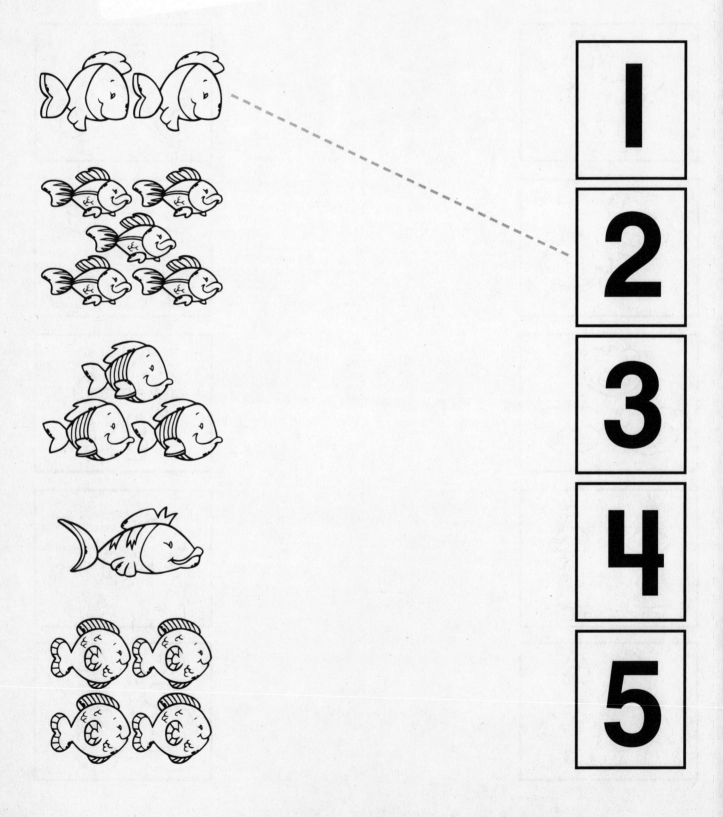

Counting to 5; matching numerals with the correct number of objects

Under the Sea

Circle the correct number.

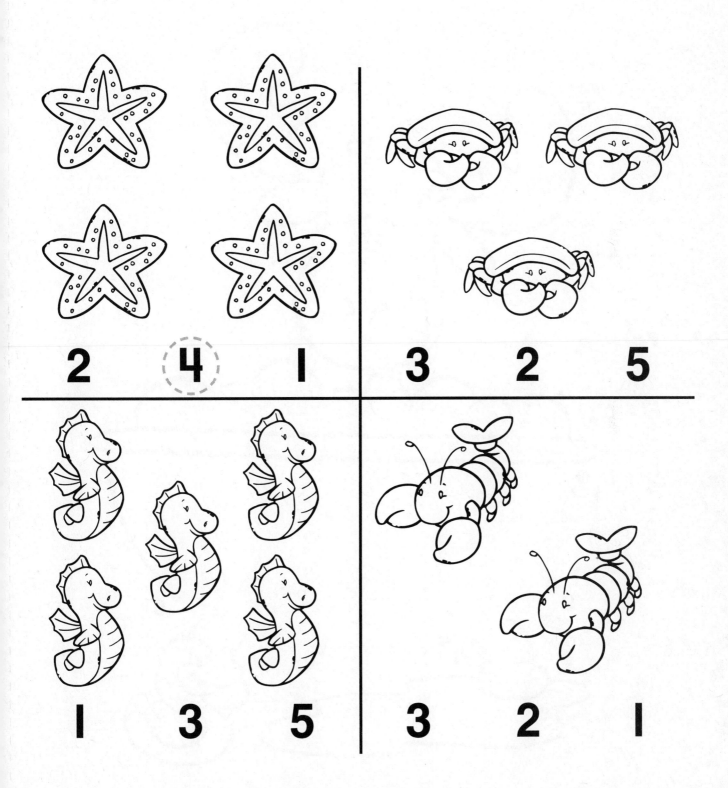

2   4   1   3   2   5

1   3   5   3   2   1

Bubble Bath Dot-to-dot

Connect the dots from **1** to **5**. Color the picture.

Understanding numerical order; developing fine motor control

Color by Number

Use the code to color the dinosaurs.

1 = yellow   2 = orange

3 = brown   4 = blue   5 = green

More

Color the one with **more.**

Understanding more and less

Less

Color the group with **less.**

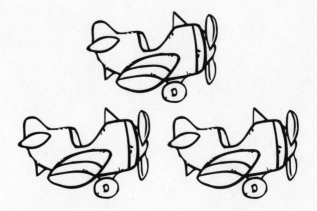

Square Deal

Trace. Draw.

square

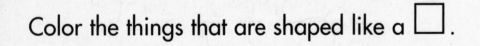

Color the things that are shaped like a ☐.

Recognizing and drawing squares

Circle It!

Trace. Draw.

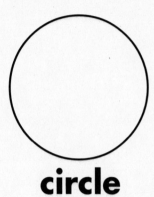

circle

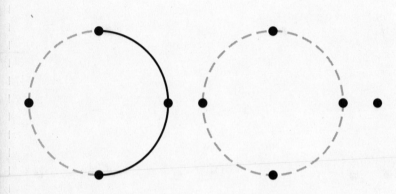

Color the things that are shaped like a ○.

Triangle Fun

Trace. Draw.

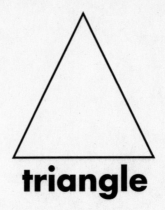

triangle

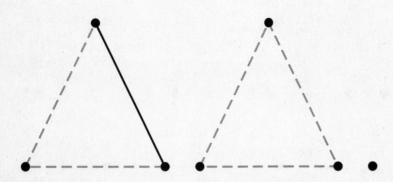 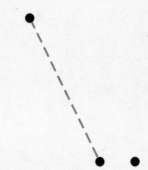

Color the things that are shaped like a △.

Ready for Rectangles!

Trace. Draw.

rectangle

Color the things that are shaped like a ☐.

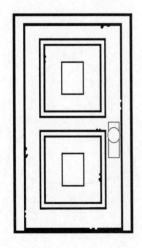

Oval Time

Trace. Draw.

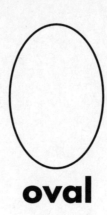

oval

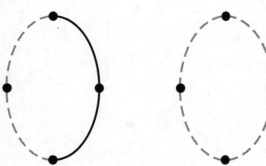

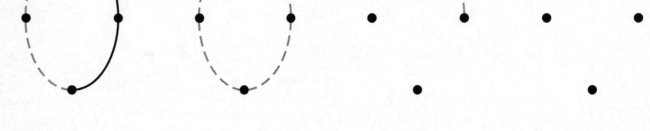

Color the things that are shaped like a ○.

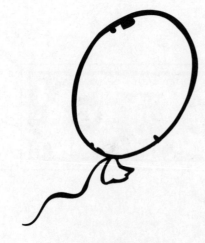

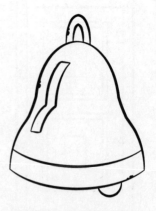

Recognizing and drawing ovals

Snack Time

Match.

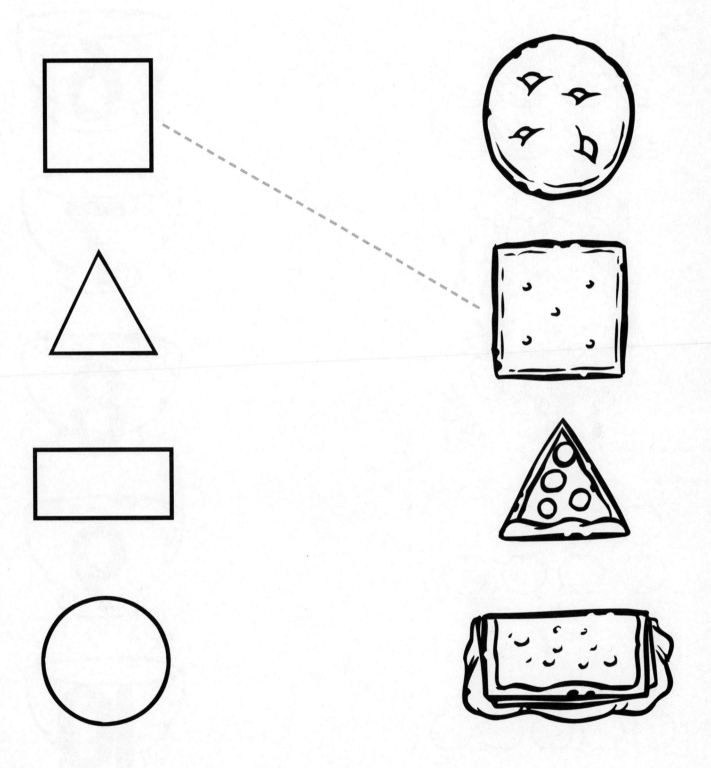

Fruit Bowls

Match.

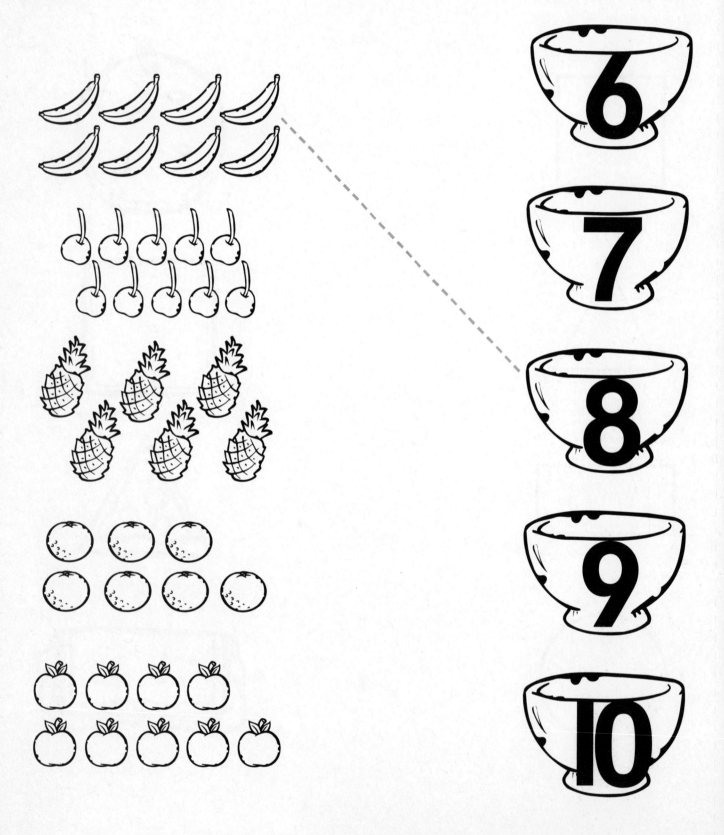

Counting to 10; matching numerals with the correct number of objects

Camping Out

Circle the correct number.

6　**7**　8

7　8　9

8　9　10

6　8　9

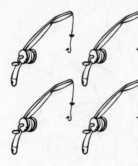

7　8　10

6　7　9

Splashing Dot-to-Dot

Connect the dots from **1** to **10**. Color the picture.

Understanding numerical order; developing fine motor control

What's Missing?

Write the missing numbers.

1 ___ 3   7 ___ 9

6 ___ 8   4 ___ 6

3 ___ 5   8 ___ 10

Sweets

1 one **2** two **3** three **4** four **5** five

Write the number word.

1

one

2

3

4

5

Writing number words

More Sweets

6 six   **7** seven   **8** eight   **9** nine   **10** ten

Write the number word.

6

7

8

9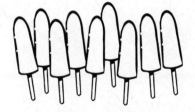

10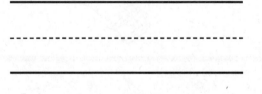

Math in Motion

Count. Write how many in all.

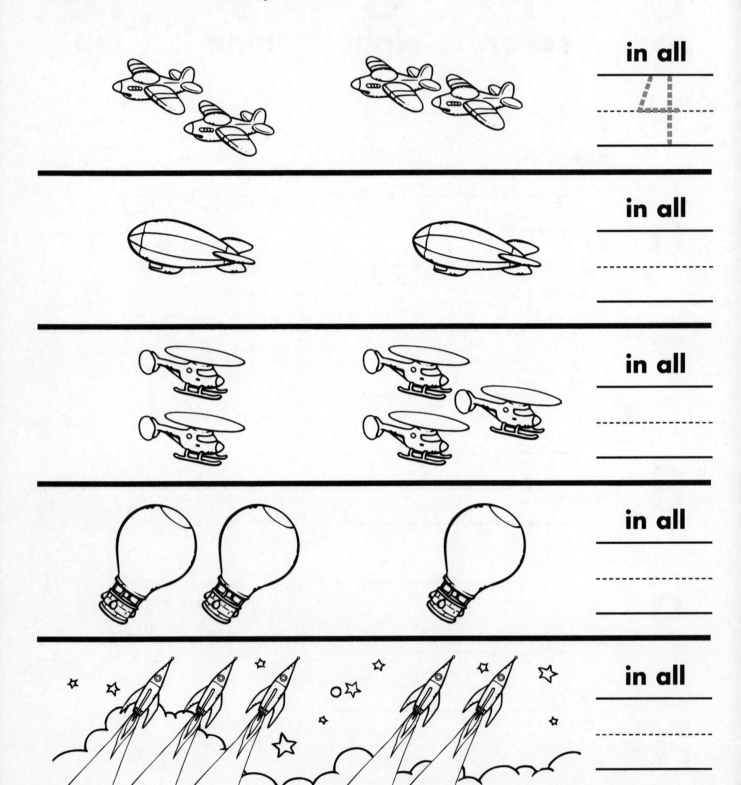

in all

4

in all

in all

in all

in all

Counting to find how many in all

Moving All Around

Count. Write how many in all.

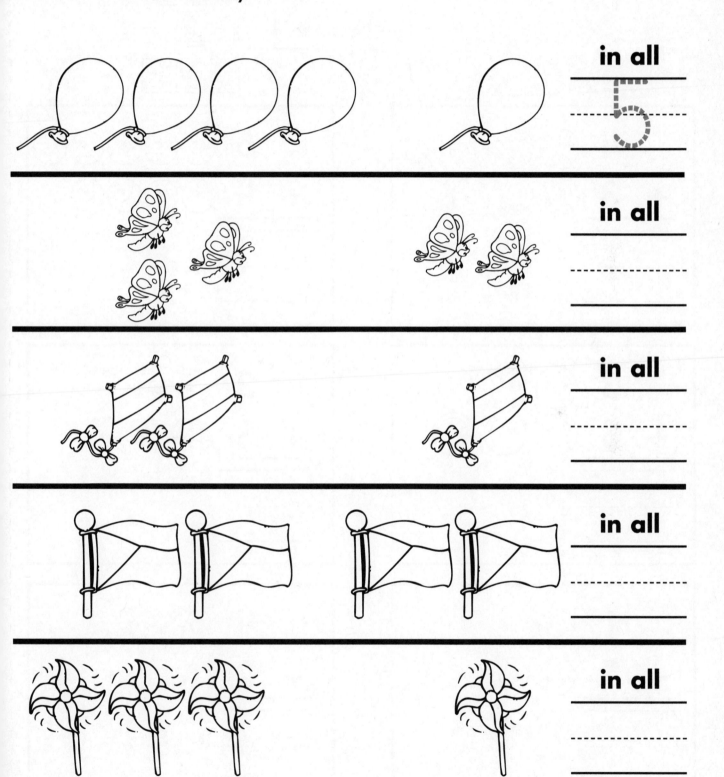

in all

in all

in all

in all

in all

Collect It

Add. Write how many.

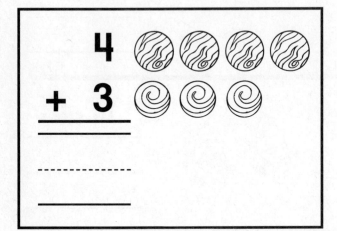

2
+ 1
―――
3

4
+ 3
――――

_____

5
+ 4
――――

_____

3
+ 3
――――

_____

2
+ 3
――――

_____

1
+ 2
――――

_____

4
+ 0
――――

_____

Adding numbers to 9

Animal Addition

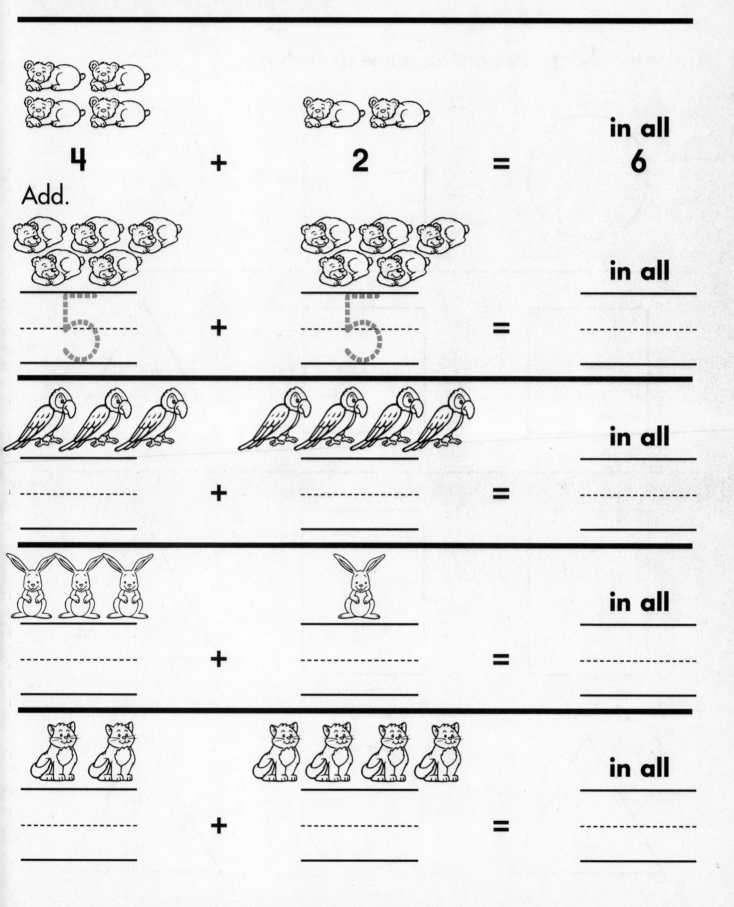

in all

4 + 2 = 6

Add.

in all

5 + 5 =

in all

____ + ____ = ____

in all

____ + ____ = ____

in all

____ + ____ = ____

Shapes in a Row

Color the shapes that are the same in each row.

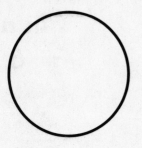  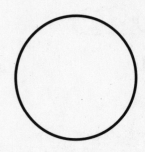

  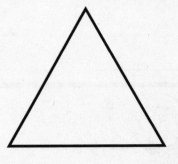

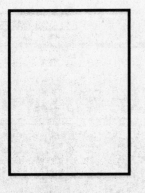 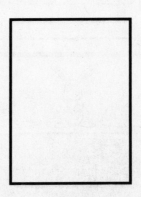 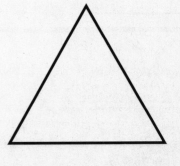

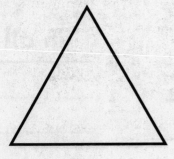 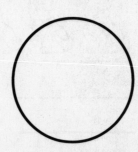 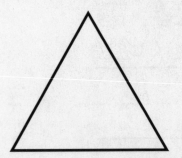

Identifying shapes

Next Shape?

Draw what comes next. Use the code to color the shapes.

 =     =

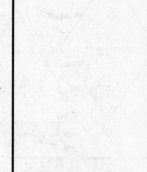

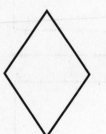 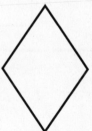  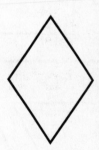

 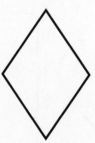 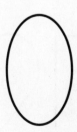 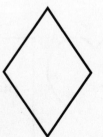 

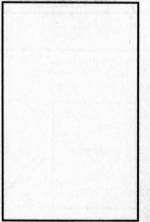

Colored Shape Patterns

Draw what comes next. Use the code to color the shapes.

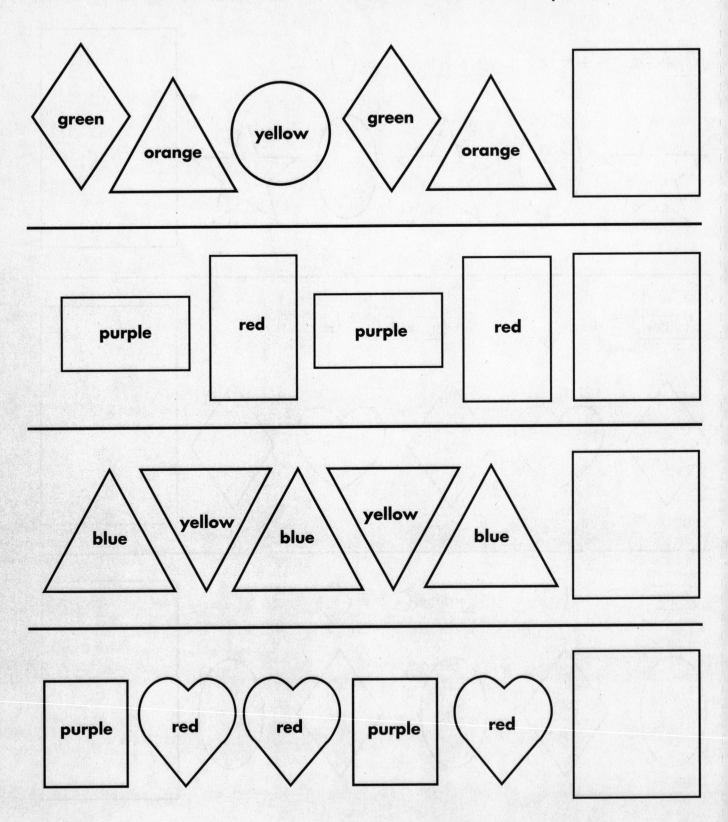

Recognizing and continuing patterns

Number Patterns

Write the next number in the pattern.

1 2 3 4 5 _6_

10 9 8 7 6 ___

4 5 6 7 8 ___

9 8 7 6 5 ___

Counting Patterns

Count and write the number.
Draw what comes next and write the number.

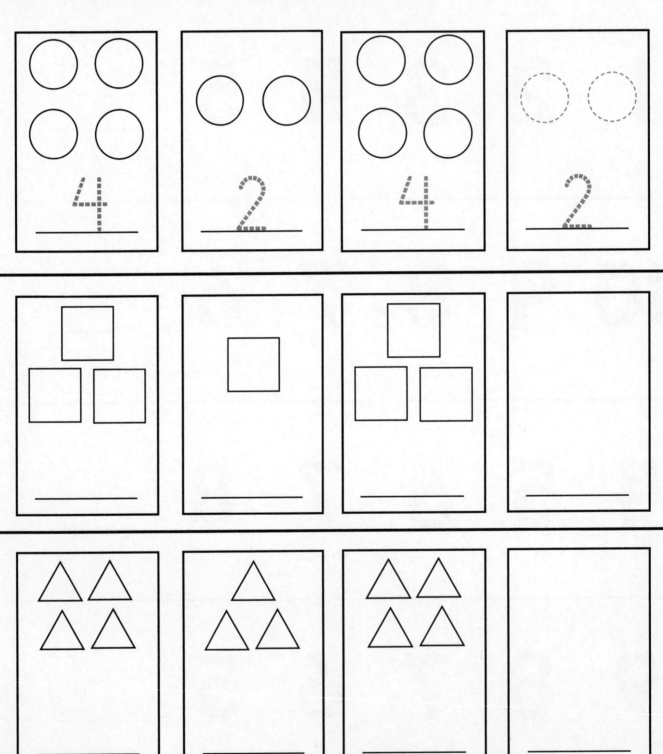

Counting; recognizing and continuing patterns

Up to 10 and Down Again!

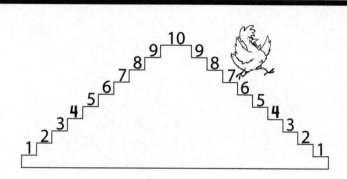

Write **1** to **10**.

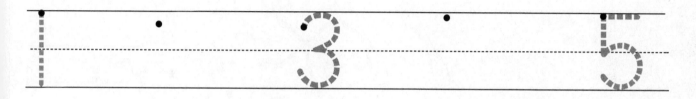

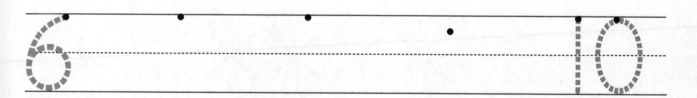

Write **10** to **1**.

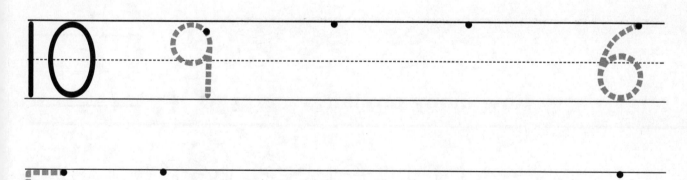

Time to Eat

Subtract.

How many are left? 4 – 2 = ____ 2

How many are left? 3 – 1 = ____

How many are left? 5 – 4 = ____

How many are left? 4 – 3 = ____

How many are left? 5 – 2 = ____

Subtracting from numbers up to 5

School Supplies

Subtract.

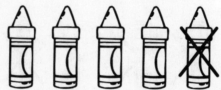

How many are left?   5 – 1 = _____

How many are left?   4 – 4 = _____

How many are left?   3 – 2 = _____

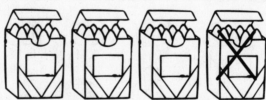

How many are left?   4 – 1 = _____

How many are left?   5 – 3 = _____

Old and New Keys

Cross out and subtract.

X out 7.

How many are left? **8 – 7 =** _____

X out 5.

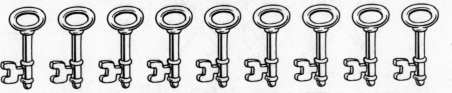

How many are left? **9 – 5 =** _____

X out 5.

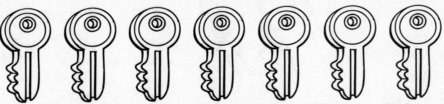

How many are left? **7 – 5 =** _____

X out 3.

How many are left? **6 – 3 =** _____

X out 2.

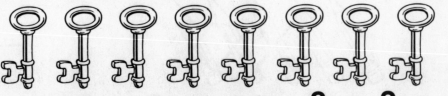

How many are left? **8 – 2 =** _____

    Subtracting from numbers up to 9

Fruit Stand

Cross out and subtract.

$$\begin{array}{r} 10 \\ -\ 5 \\ \hline \end{array}$$

How many are left? _____

X out 3.

$$\begin{array}{r} 9 \\ -\ 3 \\ \hline \end{array}$$

How many are left? _____

X out 2.

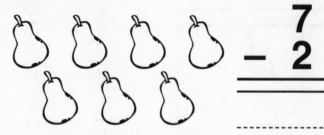

$$\begin{array}{r} 7 \\ -\ 2 \\ \hline \end{array}$$

How many are left? _____

X out 5.

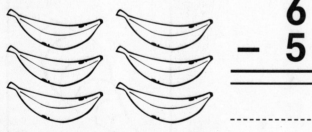

$$\begin{array}{r} 6 \\ -\ 5 \\ \hline \end{array}$$

How many are left? _____

X out 4.

$$\begin{array}{r} 10 \\ -\ 4 \\ \hline \end{array}$$

How many are left? _____

X out 8.

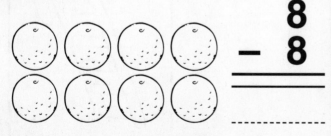

$$\begin{array}{r} 8 \\ -\ 8 \\ \hline \end{array}$$

How many are left? _____

X out 1.

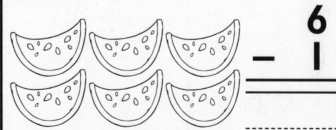

$$\begin{array}{r} 6 \\ -\ 1 \\ \hline \end{array}$$

How many are left? _____

Whole-to-Part

Match.

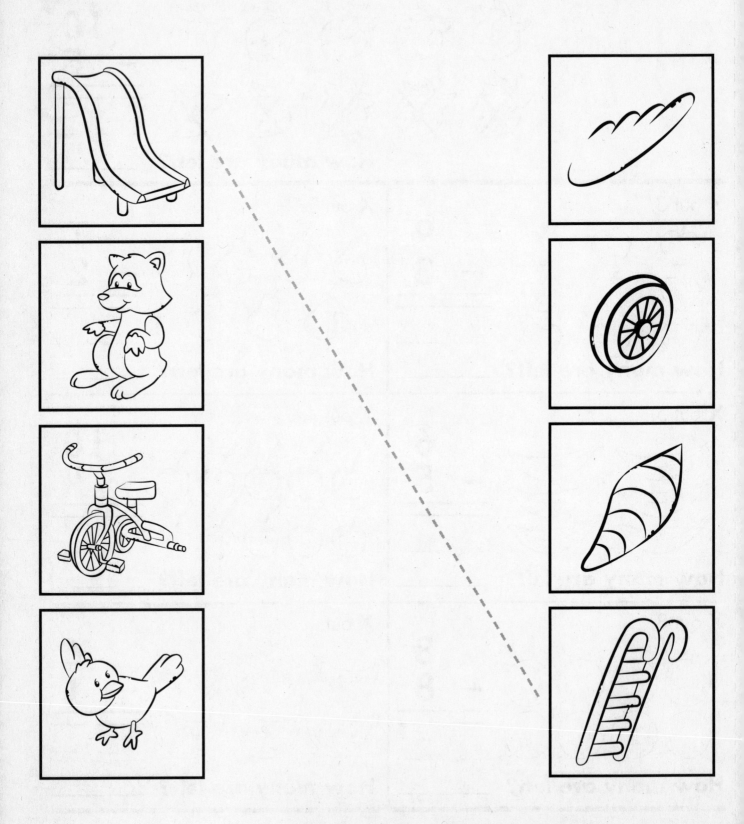

Recognizing parts of a whole

Pieces

Match.

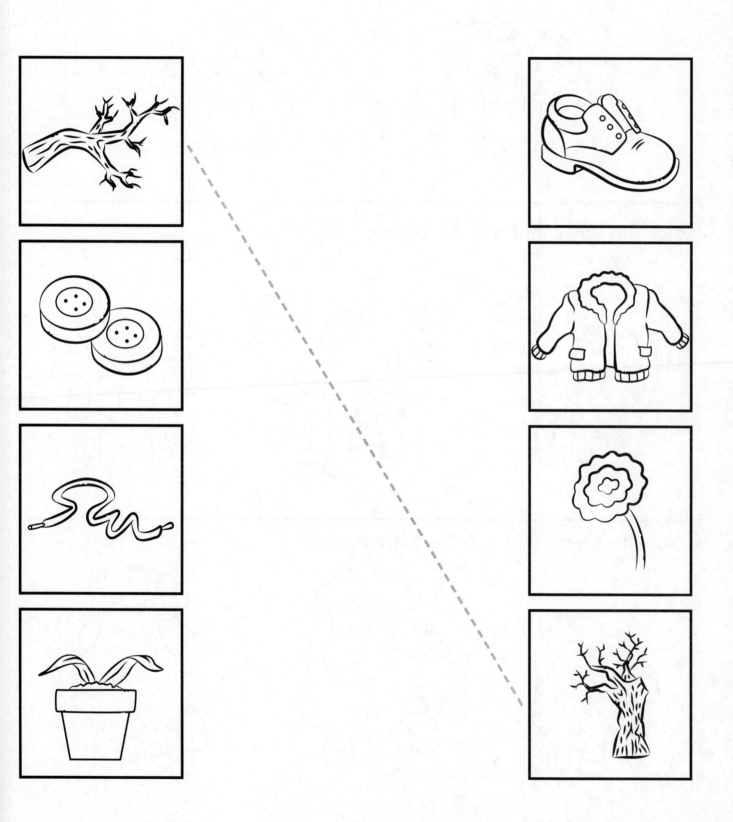

Same Size

Color the cows that are the **same** size.

Color the sheep that are the **same** size.

Understanding sizes and size words

Big and Little

Color the **big** animal. Circle the **little** animal.

Understanding sizes and size words

Longest and Shortest

Color the **longest** ones yellow. Color the **shortest** ones green.

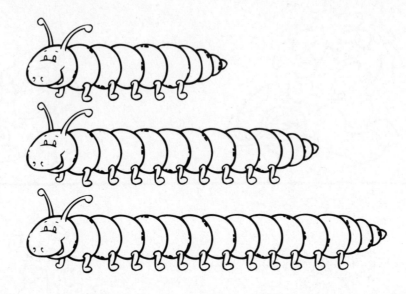

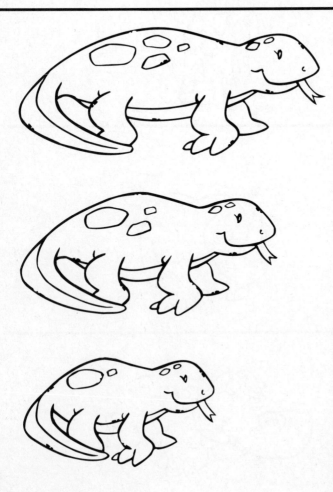

Understanding sizes and size words

Tallest and Shortest

Color the **tallest** ones red.
Color the **shortest** ones blue.

At School

11 12 13 14 15 16 17 18 19 20

Count. Write how many.

	12	

In the Sky

Match.

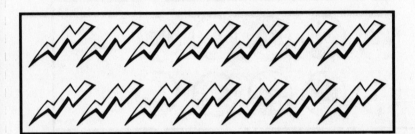

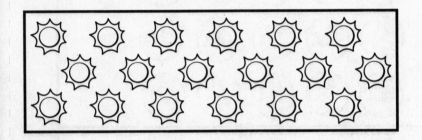

18

20

11

14

12

Counting Pennies

Color the correct number of pennies.

3 ¢	
5 ¢	
7 ¢	
10 ¢	
11 ¢	
15 ¢	

Understanding the value of a penny; Counting to 15

Tick-Tock Parts

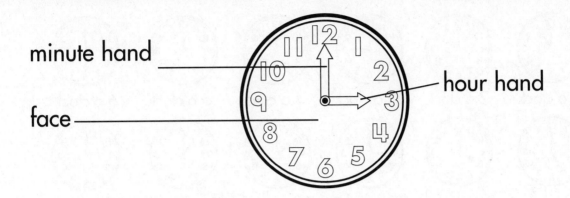

minute hand

hour hand

face

Color the **numbers** red.

Color the **hour hand** blue.

Color the **face** yellow.

Color the **minute hand** green.

All About O'Clock

1 o'clock   2 o'clock   3 o'clock   4 o'clock   5 o'clock   6 o'clock

7 o'clock   8 o'clock   9 o'clock   10 o'clock   11 o'clock   12 o'clock

Circle the correct time.

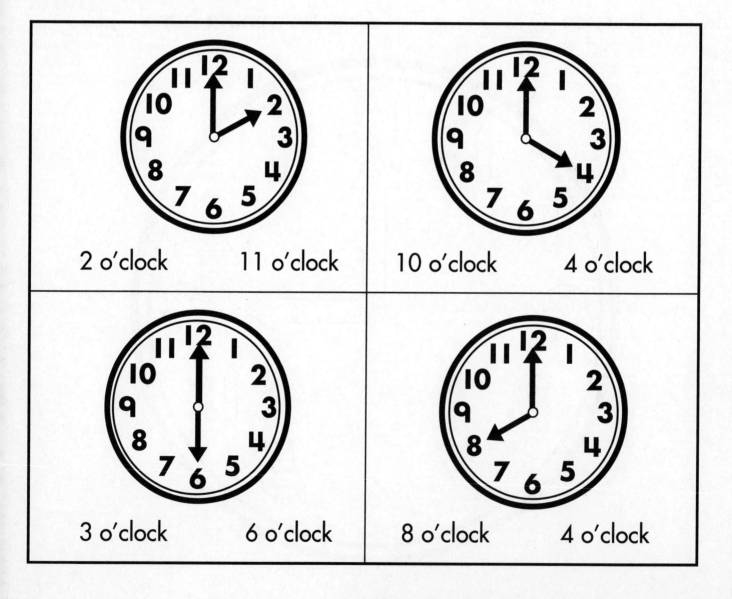

2 o'clock   11 o'clock   10 o'clock   4 o'clock

3 o'clock   6 o'clock   8 o'clock   4 o'clock

Telling time

Telling Time

3 o'clock

3:00

Write the time.

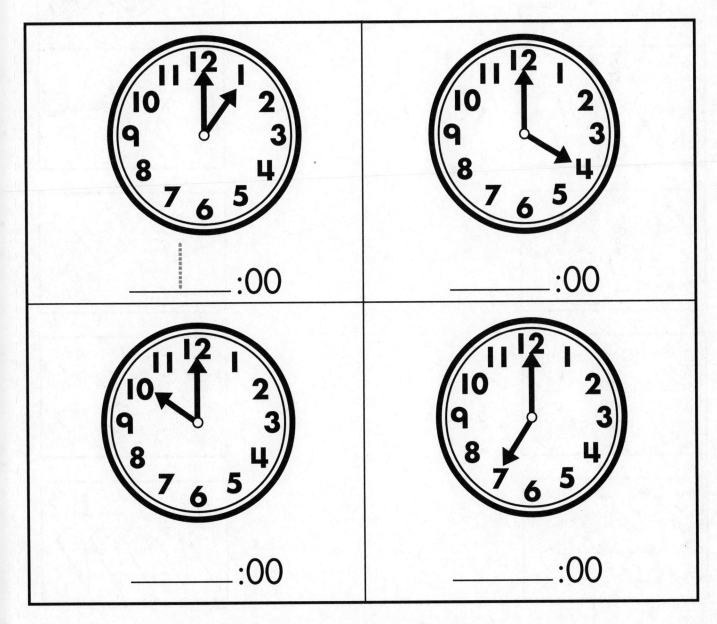

_____:00

_____:00

_____:00

_____:00

In the Garden

Match.

Matching like sets

Matching 1 to 10

Circle the correct number.

(**1**)   **2**   **3**

6   **7**   **8**

8   **9**   **10**

4   **5**   **6**

2   **3**   **4**

7   **8**   **9**

At the Zoo

Color the correct number.

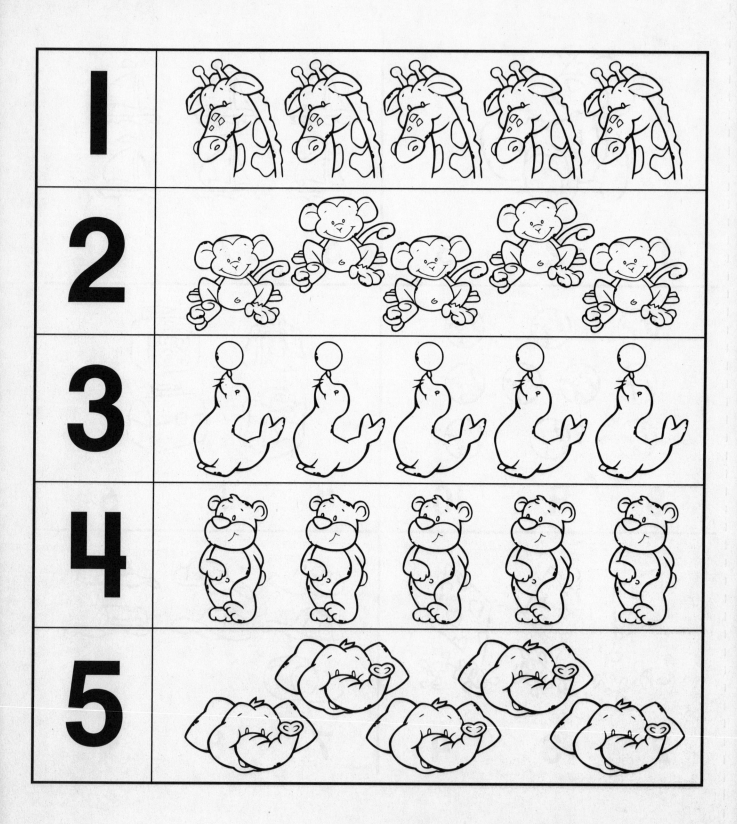

Counting to 5; matching numerals with the correct number of objects

Feathered Friends

Color the correct number.

6	
7	
8	
9	
10	

Counting to 10; matching numerals with the correct number of objects

On the Farm

Find and color the items below in the picture on the next page.
Count and circle how many.

Counting to 10; recognizing numerals

Counting to 10

More

Color the group with **more**.

Less

Color the group with **less**.

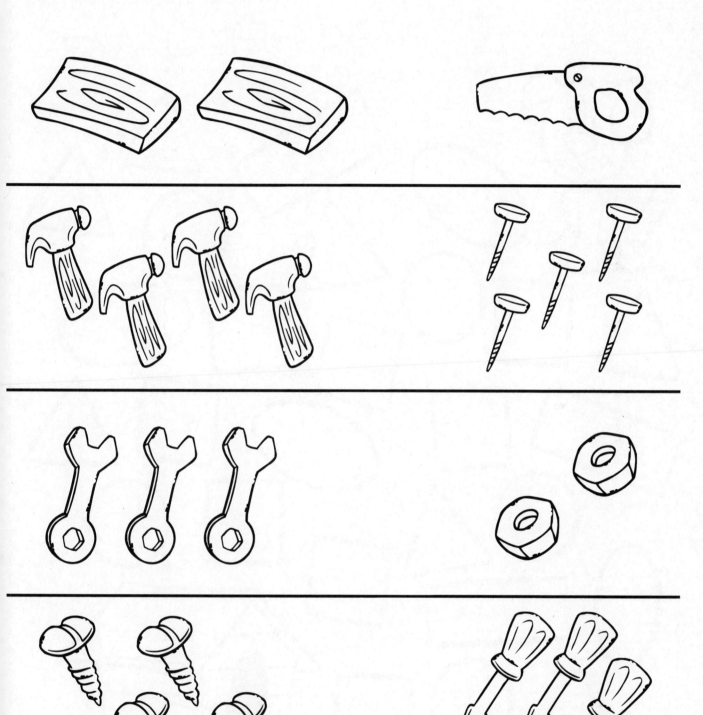

A-Maze-ing

Color the ▢s to make a path from the dog to the doghouse.

Identifying shapes

Playing Dress Up

Use the code to color the picture.

6 = orange   7 = red

8 = pink   9 = purple   10 = black

Vegetable Garden

Add.

5 + 3 = ____
____8____

4 + 2 = ____
- - - - - - - -

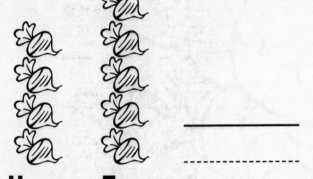

4 + 5 = ____
- - - - - - - -

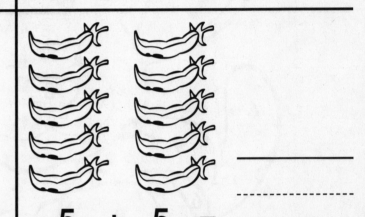

5 + 5 = ____
- - - - - - - -

2 + 3 = ____
- - - - - - - -

3 + 3 = ____
- - - - - - - -

Adding numbers to 10

Music Fun

Cross out and subtract.

X out 6.

How many are left? 10 − 6 = _____ 4

X out 4.

How many are left? 9 − 7 = _____

X out 5.

How many are left? 8 − 5 = _____

X out 8.

How many are left? 10 − 8 = _____

X out 3.

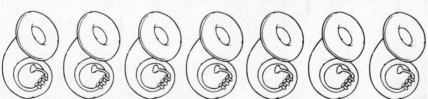

How many are left? 7 − 3 = _____

More Counting Patterns

Count and write the number.
Draw what comes next and write the number.

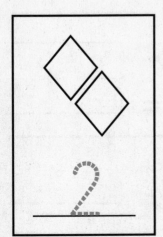

2
_____

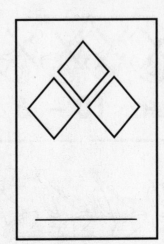

_____

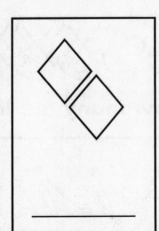

_____

_____

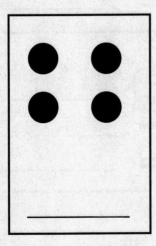

_____

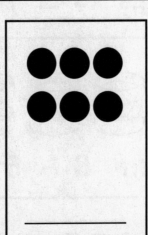

_____

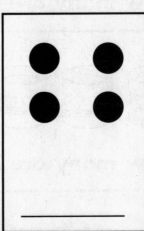

_____

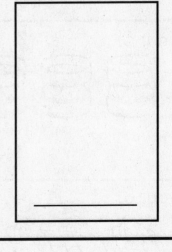

_____

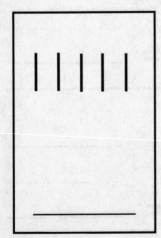

_____

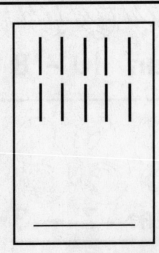

_____

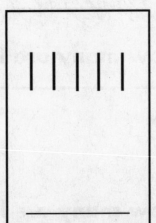

_____

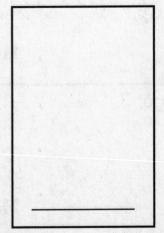

_____

Counting; recognizing and continuing patterns

Look Out Below!

Connect the dots from **1** to **20**.
Color the picture.

14 13

15 12

16 11

17 10

6

18 8

4 7 9

19 5

20 2 3 1

Understanding numerical order; developing fine motor control

59

Bzzzzy Writing Time

Write the time.

_____:00

_____:00

_____:00

_____:00

Answer Key

Please take time to review the work your child has completed and remember to praise both success and effort. If your child makes a mistake, let him or her know that mistakes are a part of learning. Then explain the correct answer and how to find it. Taking the time to help your child and an active interest in his or her progress shows that you feel learning is important.

page 1

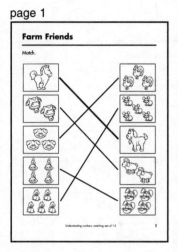

page 2

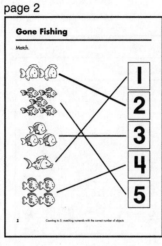

page 3

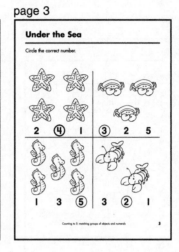

page 4

page 5

page 6

page 7

page 8

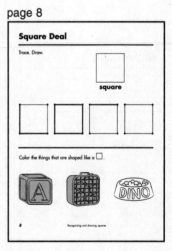

page 9

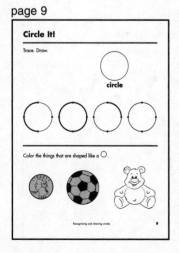

page 10

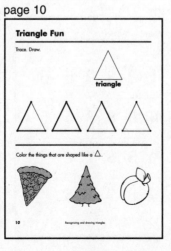

page 11

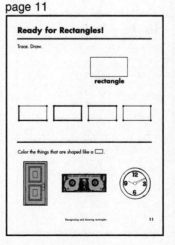

page 12

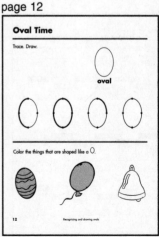

page 13

Snack Time

Match.

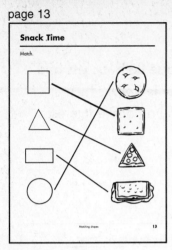

Matching shapes 13

page 14

Fruit Bowls

Match.

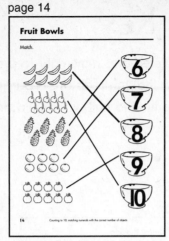

14 Counting to 10; matching numerals with the correct number of objects

page 15

Camping Out

Circle the correct number.

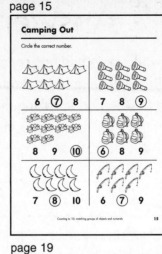

Counting to 10; matching groups of objects and numerals 15

page 16

Splashing Dot-to-Dot

Connect the dots from **1** to **10**. Color the picture.

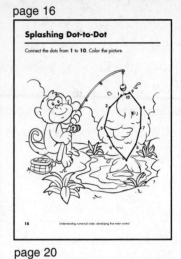

16 Understanding numerical order; developing fine motor control

page 17

What's Missing?

Write the missing numbers.

1 2 3   7 8 9

6 7 8   4 5 6

3 4 5   8 9 10

Understanding numerical order; writing numerals 17

page 18

Sweets

1	2	3	4	5
one	two	three	four	five

Write the number word.

1 **one**
2 two
3 three
4 four
5 five

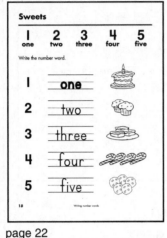

18 Writing number words

page 19

More Sweets

6	7	8	9	10
six	seven	eight	nine	ten

Write the number word.

6 **six**
7 seven
8 eight
9 nine
10 ten

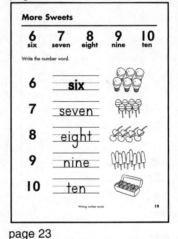

Writing number words 19

page 20

Math in Motion

Count. Write how many in all.

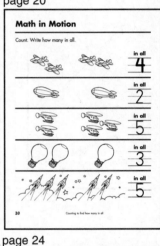

in all 4
in all 2
in all 5
in all 3
in all 5

20 Counting to find how many in all

page 21

Moving All Around

Count. Write how many in all.

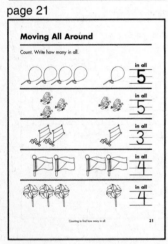

in all 5
in all 5
in all 3
in all 4
in all 4

Counting to find how many in all 21

page 22

Collect It

Add. Write how many.

```
  2
+ 1
  3
```

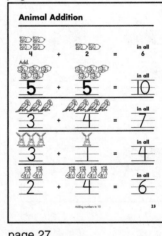

```
  4        5
+ 3      + 4
  7        9

  3        2
+ 3      + 3
  6        5

  1        4
+ 2      + 0
  3        4
```

22 Adding numbers to 9

page 23

Animal Addition

4 + 2 = in all 6

Add.

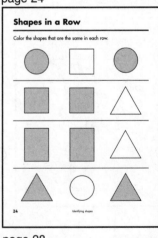

5 + 5 = 10
3 + 4 = 7
3 + 1 = 4
2 + 4 = in all 6

Adding numbers to 10 23

page 24

Shapes in a Row

Color the shapes that are the same in each row.

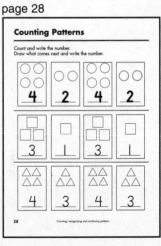

24 Identifying shapes

page 25

Next Shape?

Draw what comes next. Use the code to color the shapes.

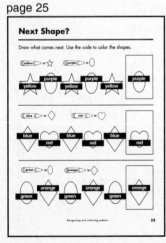

yellow purple yellow purple yellow | purple

blue red blue red blue | red

green orange green orange green | orange

Recognizing and continuing patterns 25

page 26

Colored Shape Patterns

Draw what comes next. Use the code to color the shapes.

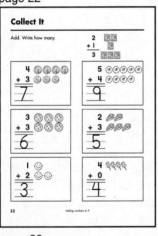

green orange yellow green orange | yellow

purple red purple red purple | red

blue yellow blue yellow blue | yellow

purple red red purple red | red

26 Recognizing and continuing patterns

page 27

Number Patterns

Write the next number in the pattern.

1 2 3 4 5 6

10 9 8 7 6 5

4 5 6 7 8 9

9 8 7 6 5 4

Counting forward and backward; recognizing number order 27

page 28

Counting Patterns

Count and write the number.
Draw what comes next and write the number.

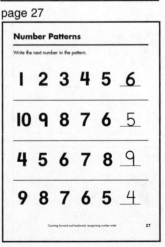

4 2 4 2

3 1 3 1

4 3 4 3

28 Counting; recognizing and continuing patterns

62

Answers

Up to 10 and Down Again!

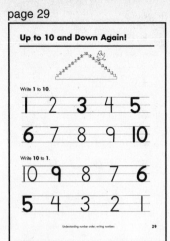

Write 1 to 10.

1 2 3 4 5
6 7 8 9 10

Write 10 to 1.

10 9 8 7 6
5 4 3 2 1

Understanding number order; writing numbers   29

Time to Eat

Subtract.

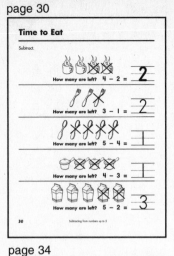

How many are left?   4 − 2 = 2
How many are left?   3 − 1 = 2
How many are left?   5 − 4 = 1
How many are left?   4 − 3 = 1
How many are left?   5 − 2 = 3

30   Subtracting from numbers up to 5

School Supplies

Subtract.

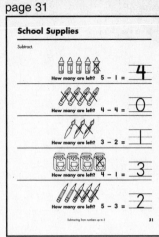

How many are left?   5 − 1 = 4
How many are left?   4 − 4 = 0
How many are left?   3 − 2 = 1
How many are left?   4 − 1 = 3
How many are left?   5 − 3 = 2

Subtracting from numbers up to 5   31

Old and New Keys

Cross out and subtract.

X out 7.   How many are left?   8 − 7 = 1
X out 5.   How many are left?   9 − 5 = 4
X out 5.   How many are left?   7 − 5 = 2
X out 3.   How many are left?   6 − 3 = 3
X out 2.   How many are left?   8 − 2 = 6

32   Subtracting from numbers up to 9

Fruit Stand

Cross out and subtract.

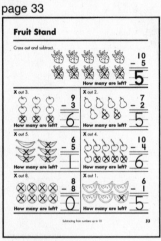

$\begin{array}{r} 10 \\ -5 \\ \hline 5 \end{array}$ How many are left?

X out 3.   How many are left? $\begin{array}{r} 9 \\ -3 \\ \hline 6 \end{array}$
X out 2.   How many are left? $\begin{array}{r} 7 \\ -2 \\ \hline 5 \end{array}$
X out 5.   How many are left? $\begin{array}{r} 6 \\ -5 \\ \hline 1 \end{array}$
X out 4.   How many are left? $\begin{array}{r} 10 \\ -4 \\ \hline 6 \end{array}$
X out 8.   How many are left? $\begin{array}{r} 8 \\ -8 \\ \hline 0 \end{array}$
X out 1.   How many are left? $\begin{array}{r} 6 \\ -1 \\ \hline 5 \end{array}$

Subtracting from numbers up to 10   33

Whole-to-Part

Match.

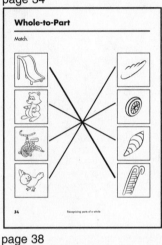

34   Recognizing parts of a whole

Pieces

Match.

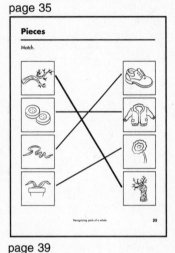

Recognizing parts of a whole   35

Same Size

Color the cows that are the **same** size.

Color the sheep that are the **same** size.

36   Understanding sizes and size words

Big and Little

Color the **big** animal. Circle the **little** animal.

Understanding sizes and size words   37

Longest and Shortest

Color the **longest** ones yellow. Color the **shortest** ones green.

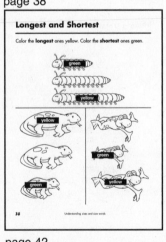

green
yellow
yellow
green
green
yellow

38   Understanding sizes and size words

Tallest and Shortest

Color the **tallest** ones red.
Color the **shortest** ones blue.

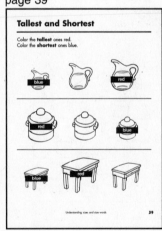

blue   red
red   blue
blue   red

Understanding sizes and size words   39

At School

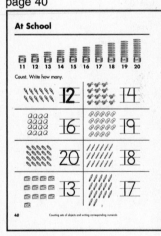

11 12 13 14 15 16 17 18 19 20

Count. Write how many.

12   14
16   19
20   18
13   17

40   Counting sets of objects and writing corresponding numerals

In the Sky

Match.

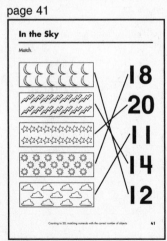

18
20
11
14
12

Counting to 20; matching numerals with the correct number of objects   41

Counting Pennies

Color the correct number of pennies.

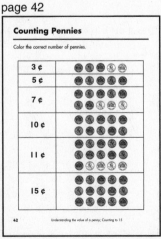

3 ¢
5 ¢
7 ¢
10 ¢
11 ¢
15 ¢

42   Understanding the value of a penny; Counting to 15

Tick-Tock Parts

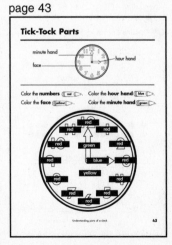

minute hand — hour hand
face

Color the **numbers** red.   Color the **hour hand** blue.
Color the **face** yellow.   Color the **minute hand** green.

red
red   red
red   green   red
blue
red   red
yellow
red   red

Understanding parts of a clock   43

All About O'Clock

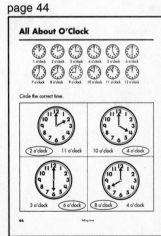

1 o'clock 2 o'clock 3 o'clock 4 o'clock 5 o'clock 6 o'clock
7 o'clock 8 o'clock 9 o'clock 10 o'clock 11 o'clock 12 o'clock

Circle the correct time.

2 o'clock   11 o'clock   10 o'clock   4 o'clock
3 o'clock   6 o'clock   8 o'clock   4 o'clock

44   Telling time

Answers

page 45

Telling Time

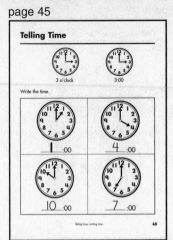

page 46

In the Garden

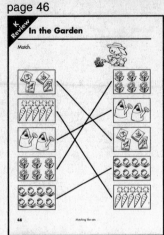

page 47

Matching 1 to 10

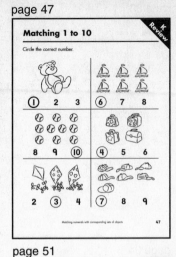

page 48

At the Zoo

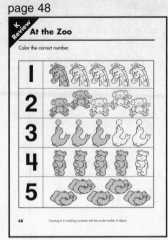

page 49

Feathered Friends

page 50

On the Farm

page 51

page 52

More

page 53

Less

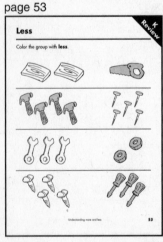

page 54

A-Maze-ing

page 55

Playing Dress Up

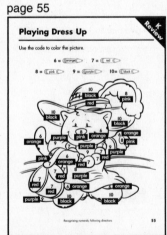

page 56

Vegetable Garden

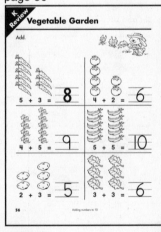

page 57

Music Fun

page 58

More Counting Patterns

page 59

Look Out Below!

page 60

Bzzzzy Writing Time

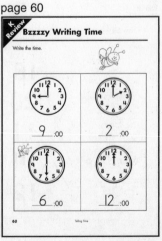